The symbols in the book tell you whether the animal is:

Vertebrate ■ or invertebrate □

Warm blooded ▲ or cold blooded △

Nocturnal ▬ or diurnal ▭

and whether the animal has babies (young born alive) ● or lays eggs ○.

If there is no symbol ▬ or ▭ it means that the animal sometimes sleeps in the day and sometimes at night.

Scientists classify animals into groups.

The animals in this encyclopaedia fit into the following groups:

mollusc	crustacean	arachnid
insect	fish	amphibian
reptile	bird	mammal

Some of the words you may not understand are explained in the glossary on page 70 in Volume 4.

Magpie

Scientific name
Pica pica

bird

■ Vertebrate ▲ Warm blooded ○ Lays eggs ▭ Diurnal

The magpie can be a thief. It likes bright shiny things. Some magpies take jewellery from open windows. Magpies also steal and eat the eggs from other birds' nests.

Adult size to scale

| 0 | 25 | 50 | 75 | 1 metre |

Home
Woodland, parks, gardens.
Nests in trees.

Young
5 to 8 blue-green eggs.

Food
Insects, scraps, other birds' eggs.

Mole

Scientific name
Talpa europaea

mammal

■ Vertebrate ▲ Warm blooded ● Young born alive

Moles live under the ground in dark tunnels. Their strong front legs, claws and flat paws make them very good at digging. They do not need good eyesight. They use their sense of smell to find their way around.

Adult size to scale

| 0 | 25 | 50 | 75 | 1 metre |

Home
Grassland, woodland, gardens.

Young
3 to 4 babies born underground.

Food
Worms, insects.

Mosquito

Scientific name
Aedes punctor

insect

☐ Invertebrate   △ Cold blooded   ○ Lays eggs

The mosquito is an insect which lives near water. It is also called a gnat. The female bites and sucks the blood of animals and people. The male mosquito does not eat blood. It sucks the juices of plants.

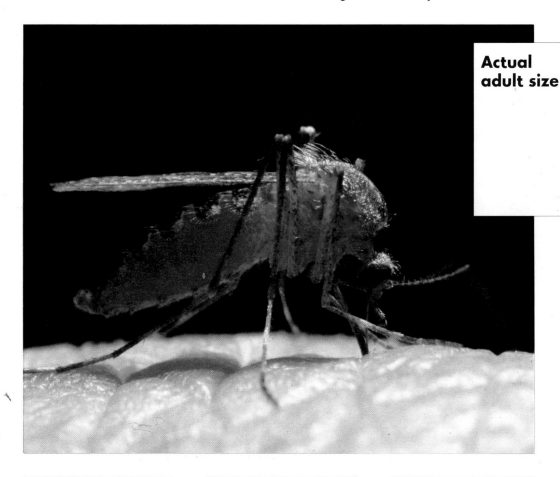

Actual adult size

Home
Woodland, gardens, damp places.

Young
Hundreds of eggs laid on top of water. Young mosquitoes live in water.

Food
Females eat blood. Males eat plant juices. Young eat tiny bits of plants in the water.

36

Moth

Large yellow underwing

Scientific name

Noctua pronuba

insect

□ Invertebrate △ Cold blooded ○ Lays eggs ▬ Nocturnal

This moth has brown front wings and bright yellow back wings. It can tuck its bright wings away so that it is camouflaged. It can also open its wings quickly to make a flash of colour. This can frighten predators.

Adult size to scale

0 25 50 75 1 metre

Home

Parks, gardens.

Young

Lays 200 eggs.

Food

Nectar from flowers.

Mouse

Woodmouse

Scientific name
Apodemus sylvaticus

mammal

■ Vertebrate ▲ Warm blooded ● Young born alive ▨ Nocturnal

There are lots of woodmice in Britain. They have big ears so they can hear if danger is near. They gnaw and eat all sorts of things. Sometimes they will even eat each other.

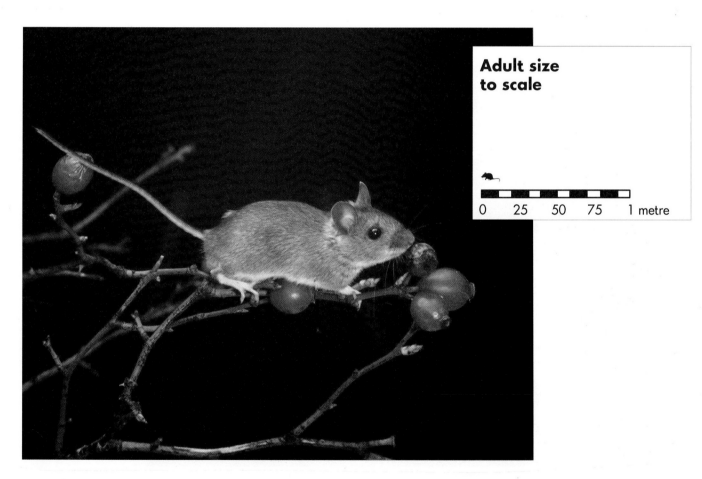

Adult size to scale

0   25   50   75   1 metre

Home
Meadows, sand-dunes, gardens, woodland. Lives in underground burrow.

Young
4 to 5 babies born underground. Babies born blind with no fur.

Food
Nuts, berries, seeds, buds, snails, scraps.

Mussel

Edible mussel

Scientific name
Mytilis edulis

mollusc

☐ Invertebrate   △ Cold blooded   ○ Lays eggs

Mussels make a sticky string which they use to stick themselves to rock. They suck in sea water which has tiny bits of food in it. Larger animals and people eat mussels.

Actual adult size

Home
Sea. On rocks.

Young
Millions of eggs laid in sea. Very young mussels swim about.

Food
Tiny bits of plants and animals in the sea.

Newt

Common Newt

Scientific name
Triturus vulgaris

amphibian

■ Vertebrate △ Cold blooded ○ Lays eggs

The newt can live in water or on land. When it grows it needs a newer bigger skin so it sheds its old skin. It leaves the old skin behind or eats it up.

Adult size to scale

| 0 | 25 | 50 | 75 | 1 metre |

Home
Ponds, damp places. Hibernates under logs and stones.

Young
200 to 300 eggs laid singly in water.

Food
Slugs, worms, insects, water fleas.

Otter

Scientific name
Lutra lutra

mammal

■ Vertebrate ▲ Warm blooded ● Young born alive ▬ Nocturnal

Otters have long thin bodies, webbed feet and thick tails which all help to make them good swimmers. They need to live near clean water with plenty of fish to eat. There are fewer otters nowadays because so much water is very dirty.

Adult size to scale

0   25   50   75   1 metre

Home
Rivers, the seaside.
Makes den (called a holt) in bank.

Young
2 to 3 babies born in the holt.

Food
Fish, mussels, crabs.

41

Owl

Barn owl

Scientific name
Tyto alba

bird

 Vertebrate   ▲ Warm blooded   ◯ Lays eggs   Nocturnal

The barn owl hunts at night. It can hear and see very well. It flies silently, to find a small tasty animal. Then it swoops and uses its sharp claws to kill and pick up its prey.

Adult size to scale.

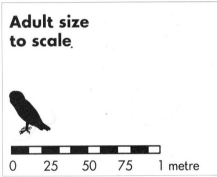

| 0 | 25 | 50 | 75 | 1 metre |

Home
Open land.
Nests in hollow trees and barns.

Young
3 to 11 white eggs.

Food
Insects, frogs, mice, other small animals.

Oyster

Edible oyster

Scientific name
Ostrea edulis

mollusc

☐ Invertebrate △ Cold blooded ◯ Lays eggs

Oysters can open and close their shells when they want to eat. When young oysters are ready to be born, the female opens her shell and blows out clouds of baby oysters.

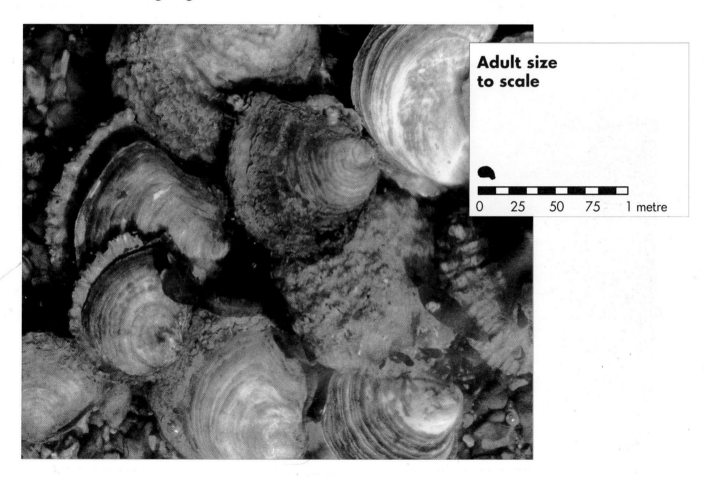

Adult size to scale

0 25 50 75 1 metre

Home
Bottom of sea. Oyster beds.

Young
1 million eggs. Babies born male. Then they become female.

Food
Very tiny bits of plants and animals in the water.

Pike

Scientific name
Esox lucius

fish

■ Vertebrate   △ Cold blooded   ○ Lays eggs

The pike is a large and fierce fish. It has sharp teeth. It hides in the water weeds, where it is camouflaged by its golden spots. Then it attacks its prey. Big pike have attacked and eaten rats, ducks and even swans.

Adult size to scale

0   25   50   75   1 metre

Home
Rivers and lakes.

Young
Female lays up to half a million eggs at a time.

Food
Fish, frogs, animals and birds.

44

Pond skater

Scientific name
Gerris lacustris

insect

☐ Invertebrate　　△ Cold blooded　　◯ Lays eggs

The pond skater lives on the top of lakes or ponds.
It rows with its legs and moves very fast. It catches
insects that fall into the water and sucks all the
juices out of their bodies.

Actual adult size

Home
Ponds and lakes.

Young
100 eggs laid
on underwater plants.

Food
Insects.

Rabbit

Scientific name
Oryctolagus cuniculus

mammal

■ Vertebrate ▲ Warm blooded ● Young born alive

Rabbits live in groups and sleep underground. They come up and nibble grass but they hop down a hole if they are frightened. The bobbing of their white tails is a signal to other rabbits that danger is near.

Adult size to scale

0   25   50   75   1 metre

Home
Open grassland.
Lives in a warren of underground tunnels.

Young
3 to 7 babies at a time, 2 or 3 times a year.

Food
Grass. Also eats its own droppings.

Rat

Brown rat

Scientific name
Rattus norvegius

mammal

■ Vertebrate ▲ Warm blooded ● Young born alive

Rats eat almost anything. Sometimes they steal human food and they make it dirty and spread germs. Female rats have many babies. They can have them every six weeks. Rats can climb, swim and dig so they can live almost anywhere.

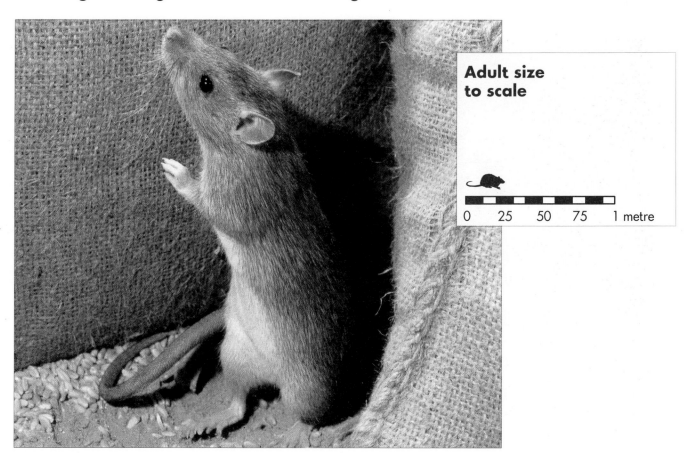

Adult size to scale

| 0 | 25 | 50 | 75 | 1 metre |

Home
Almost anywhere.

Young
7 to 11 babies
in a litter.

Food
Anything.

Robin

Scientific name
Erithacus rubecula

bird

■ Vertebrate   ▲ Warm blooded   ○ Lays eggs   ▭ Diurnal

Male robins each have a patch of land to themselves. This is called their territory. Robins fight each other to protect their territory. Their red breasts and loud singing warn other robins to keep away.

Adult size to scale

0   25   50   75   1 metre

Home
Woodland, parks, gardens.
Nests in trees, garages, holes, even old boots.

Young
5 to 6 eggs, white with red markings.

Food
Worms, insects.